# BE A LEADER

# LEADERSHIP AT SCHOOL

BY JAMES HANCOCK

BLUE OWL
BOOKS

# TIPS FOR CAREGIVERS

Leadership can be an intimidating and abstract concept. Finding ways to encourage small, everyday examples of leadership can help instill the traits of a good leader in young readers. It is important to know that there are many leadership traits, forms of leadership, and types of leaders. By helping young people identify all of the possibilities, you can help them find which types of leaders they want to be. Learning how to demonstrate the traits of a leader is a form of social and emotional learning (SEL).

## BEFORE READING

Talk to the reader about leadership.

**Discuss:** What does leadership mean to you? Who are some leaders in your life? How do they lead?

## AFTER READING

Talk to the reader about how he or she can practice leadership.

**Discuss:** What can you do at school to practice different types of leadership? What leadership traits can you develop to be a better leader?

## SEL GOAL

Young readers may have a hard time seeing themselves as leaders. Lead students in a discussion about times that they positively influenced someone or something. Discuss the leadership traits in this book. Have students think of times they have used these traits. Help them start to identify leadership traits in themselves.

# TABLE OF CONTENTS

# CHAPTER 1

# WHAT IS LEADERSHIP?

There is a new student in Tim's class. He offers to show her around and introduce her to other students. Tim shows he is a leader!

Leadership involves guiding others. Leaders positively **influence** people and their communities! Teachers, principals, and coaches all have different **roles**. But they are all leaders. Everyone can be a leader at school!

We see leadership **traits** through others' actions. Paul stands up for others at school. Joe helps solve arguments. They both make an effort to work well with others.

Liv organizes a game for her class at recess! She **includes** everyone. She doesn't tell anybody they can't play. She brings people together!

Leo **volunteers**. He is a crossing guard before and after school. This is a special **responsibility**. He helps keep people safe in the crosswalk!

## ROLE MODELS

Do you have **role models** in your life? Who are they, and how do they lead? What traits do they show? How can you be like them?

# CHAPTER 2

# LEADERS LISTEN

Leaders listen to others. Zane is in charge of directing the school play! He shares his ideas and asks everyone else to also.

Zane discovers new and exciting ideas from each person. Everyone feels involved. They all feel heard. Together, they make the play better! This is **rewarding** for everyone!

Eve's friends disagree about a game's rules. She helps solve the **conflict** by listening. She listens to each person's side. She helps explain the rules. Everyone understands each other. Eve's friends agree to play by the same rules!

When we listen carefully to others, we can get to know them. They feel understood. This helps them feel good about themselves. It can help them feel more **confident**. It builds trust, too.

## LEADERS LEARN

Listening lets you learn what people do and don't like. When you know what people like, you can lead them better. For example, some people like trying new things. Other people like to watch for a while before trying something new.

Is someone being bullied? Show you are a leader by **advocating** for that person. Stand up for people who have trouble standing up for themselves. Tell the bully that his or her actions or words are not OK. Go with your friend to talk to the teacher about the bully.

## ASK FOR HELP

Leaders advocate for themselves, too. They speak up. Do you need help with homework? Ask for help! Maybe others cut in front of you in line. Politely ask them to take their place behind you.

# CHAPTER 3

# BE A LEADER!

Leaders are always looking for ways to use their leadership skills. Bobby volunteers to lead **meditation** before class. Kim helps collect equipment after gym.

Beth's class gets a pet! She takes the lead in feeding it each day. Volunteering helps her teacher. And she gets to use her leadership skills!

Leadership helps us all feel more confident. It can create new friendships! It can help you do incredible things that couldn't be done alone.

Being a leader can be hard! It takes time and effort. But it is rewarding. How will you be a leader at school?

## SPEAK UP!

Get comfortable using your **leadership voice**! What does using your leadership voice mean? It's when you use your power as a leader to do good. You speak up for yourself and others!

# GOALS AND TOOLS

## GROW WITH GOALS

Anyone can be a leader! By showing your leadership traits at school, you can make friends, feel more confident, and have a positive impact on your school community.

**Goal:** The next time you are playing a game at school, invite someone new to join. Can you include someone new once a day?

**Goal:** Listening is a leadership trait that can be very hard. Try it out by asking people to share their opinions, asking good questions, and repeating their ideas back to make sure you understand.

**Goal:** If you see peers being treated unfairly at school, step in and help their voices be heard. Ask them how you can help advocate for them. Maybe they want to advocate for themselves. Stand with them while they do.

## WRITING REFLECTION

Make a list of situations in which you might be able to help others by using your leadership traits. During the school week, keep track of times when you use these leadership skills. Count them up at the end of the week. Can you do more the next week?

1. What are some ways you could include others at school?

2. What are some school situations in which you can help others by listening?

3. What are some ways you might be able to advocate for someone at school?

# GLOSSARY

**advocating**
Acting in support of a person, cause, or group.

**confident**
Having a strong belief in your own abilities.

**conflict**
A serious and usually lengthy disagreement.

**includes**
Welcomes.

**influence**
To have an effect on someone or something.

**leadership voice**
Using the power of your opinion and influence when you are the leader, often by using your actual voice to speak up.

**meditation**
The act of thinking deeply and quietly.

**responsibility**
A duty or job.

**rewarding**
Offering or bringing satisfaction.

**role models**
People whose behaviors in certain areas are imitated by others.

**roles**
Jobs or purposes of people or things in particular situations.

**traits**
Qualities or characteristics that make people different from each other.

**volunteers**
Offers to do a job without pay.

# TO LEARN MORE

**FACT SURFER**

## Finding more information is as easy as 1, 2, 3.

1. Go to www.factsurfer.com

2. Enter "**leadershipatschool**" into the search box.

3. Choose your cover to see a list of websites.

# INDEX

Blue Owl Books are published by Jump!, 5357 Penn Avenue South, Minneapolis, MN 55419, www.jumplibrary.com

Library of Congress Cataloging-in-Publication Data

Names: Hancock, James, author.
Title: Leadership at school / by James Hancock.
Description: Blue owl books. | Minneapolis, MN : Jump!, [2020]
Series: Be a leader | Includes index. | Audience: Ages 7–10.
Identifiers: LCCN 2019038027 (print)
LCCN 2019038028 (ebook)
ISBN 9781645272298 (hardcover)
ISBN 9781645272304 (paperback)
ISBN 9781645272311 (ebook)
Subjects: LCSH: Leadership in children–Juvenile literature.
Students–Juvenile literature. | Leadership–Juvenile literature.
Classification: LCC BF723.L4 H363 2020 (print) | LCC BF723.L4 (ebook) | DDC 303.3/4083–dc23
LC record available at https://lccn.loc.gov/2019038027
LC ebook record available at https://lccn.loc.gov/2019038028

Editor: Susanne Bushman
Designer: Jenna Casura

Photo Credits: FatCamera/iStock, cover, 4; skynesher/iStock, 1; Ridofranz/iStock, 3; monkeybusinessimages/iStock, 5; Wavebreakmedia/iStock, 6–7; Steve Skjold/Alamy, 8–9; adamkaz/iStock, 10, 11; chrispecoraro/iStock, 12–13; Brocreative/Shutterstock, 14–15; LSOphoto/iStock, 16–17; TinnaPong/Shutterstock, 18; kate_sept2004/iStock, 19; SDI Productions/iStock, 20–21.

Printed in the United States of America at Corporate Graphics in North Mankato, Minnesota.